Sexual Mathematics

# Sexual Mathematics

by Talim Arab

BRIDGES
PUBLISHING

Published by
*Bridges Publishing*
www.maurer.press

ISBN 978-3-929345-89-6

For Isaac Ryan
& C. Ward

Also by Talim Arab:
*The Square-Shaped Tear*

*"I can calculate the motion of heavenly bodies,
but not the madness of people."*

Isaac Newton

# Contents

1.  Equal relationships are indivisible by three. . . . . . . . . . 13
2.  When points belong to something at a fixed time,
    it is a date. . . . . . . . . . . . . . . . . . . . . . . . . . . . . . . . . . . . . 14
3.  The marriage bed is a sacred surface. . . . . . . . . . . . . . 15
4.  Did the imagination conceive Time? . . . . . . . . . . . . . . 16
5.  Bodies in geometric space are subject to linear time. . . . 18
6.  Memory is a line that repeats upon itself. . . . . . . . . . . . 19
7.  To formulate the proposition. . . . . . . . . . . . . . . . . . . . . 21
8.  Theorem: Economic rationalism and philosophy are
    incongruent. . . . . . . . . . . . . . . . . . . . . . . . . . . . . . . . . . 23
9.  An acute conversation: speakers are < 90°apart. . . . . . 25
10. Memory is a line that intersects with itself. . . . . . . . . . . 27
11. Like formulae, can love be re-arranged? . . . . . . . . . . . . 28
12. To propose the formula ... . . . . . . . . . . . . . . . . . . . . . . 29
13. Indifference: two circles that touch but do not
    cut one another. . . . . . . . . . . . . . . . . . . . . . . . . . . . . . . 30
14. To go beyond the proposition. . . . . . . . . . . . . . . . . . . . 31
15. Acute memories can permeate 90% of one's life. . . . . . 32
16. Definition: Bases are those who support a top. . . . . . . . 34
17. An idea is that which has depth and a vast length and
    breadth expandable over the distance of time. . . . . . . . 35
18. Let ballet be a mathematical catalyst. . . . . . . . . . . . . . 36
19. Definition: Body chronology can be unequal
    to the mind's. . . . . . . . . . . . . . . . . . . . . . . . . . . . . . . . . 37

20. Parallel planes in unparalleled spaces are those which can meet. . . . . . . . . . . . . . . . . . . . . . . . . . . . . . . . . . . 38

21. The reconciliation of parallel lines, like opposing concepts, cannot occur. . . . . . . . . . . . . . . . . . . . . . . . 40

22. When uneven planes collide, the weaker will no doubt be crushed. . . . . . . . . . . . . . . . . . . . . . . . . . . . . . . . 41

23. Two points may exist in the same space but not necessarily in the same plane. . . . . . . . . . . . . . . . . . . . . 42

24. If there is no action a consequence can still occur. . . . . 43

25. The line of compassion can filter through a phone call. . . . . . . . . . . . . . . . . . . . . . . . . . . . . . . . 44

26. The face of a solid is a surface, but a surface is not necessarily solid. . . . . . . . . . . . . . . . . . . . . . . . . . . . . 45

27. The line of compassion cannot filter through a phone call. . . . . . . . . . . . . . . . . . . . . . . . . . . . . . . . 47

28. Water abstracts the straight line. . . . . . . . . . . . . . . . . . 49

29. Let Mathematics be the bridge to the Arts. . . . . . . . . . . 51

30. Postulate1: To calculate lust. . . . . . . . . . . . . . . . . . . . . 52

31. Theorem: Love and sex coincide with one another but are not equal. . . . . . . . . . . . . . . . . . . . . . . . . . . . . 53

32. The past is that which has length and lingers. . . . . . . . . 55

33. Death's axis can be difficult to cross. . . . . . . . . . . . . . . 56

34. Love's only axiom is uncertainty. . . . . . . . . . . . . . . . . . 57

35. L ($\in$) = K $\in$ $^{1-D}$ . . . . . . . . . . . . . . . . . . . . . . . . . . . . . 58

36. For every triangle there is a sin. . . . . . . . . . . . . . . . . . . 59

37. The axiom of decision can only be made in fixed space and time. . . . . . . . . . . . . . . . . . . . . . . . . . . . . . 61

38. New angles change perspective. . . . . . . . . . . . . . . . . . 63

39. And deception is the centre of silence. . . . . . . . . . . . . . 65

*Poetics of a Mathematician I – XIV* . . . . . . . . . . . . . . . . . . . . . 67

40. The action cannot be undone. . . . . . . . . . . . . . . . . . . . 81
41. The diameter of decision can encompass
    a whole life. . . . . . . . . . . . . . . . . . . . . . . . . . . . . . . . . . . 82
42. Once bisected a life cannot be reconnected. . . . . . . . . . 83
43. Proposition: Ratios of difference may sometimes
    be equal. . . . . . . . . . . . . . . . . . . . . . . . . . . . . . . . . . . . . . 85
44. If the interval is prolonged indefinitely, the given points
    may never meet. . . . . . . . . . . . . . . . . . . . . . . . . . . . . . . . 87
45. Postulate: Death is disclosed. . . . . . . . . . . . . . . . . . . . . 88
46. Equal circles are those who interests are parallel and
    unconflicting. . . . . . . . . . . . . . . . . . . . . . . . . . . . . . . . . . 90
47. A plane angle is the inclination of two lines in a plane
    which meet one another, do not lie in a straight line,
    but lie in sympathy. . . . . . . . . . . . . . . . . . . . . . . . . . . . . . 91
48. The discourse of mathematics and medicine
    may conflict. . . . . . . . . . . . . . . . . . . . . . . . . . . . . . . . . . . 93
49. The final postulate cannot be proven. . . . . . . . . . . . . . . 94
50. A life is a line with eternal breadth. . . . . . . . . . . . . . . . 95

About the author . . . . . . . . . . . . . . . . . . . . . . . . . . . . . . . . . 97

# 1.   Equal relationships are indivisible by three.

"You came to the wrong conference, René."
"Yes, Doctor Dempewolf."
"Please, Diego. Drink?"

René refused, already intoxicated by Diego's triangular figure.
"What are you studying?" Diego asked, noticing a diary
        beside René.
"A doctorate in analytic geometry; my supervisor's
        passionately *ruthless*!"

Diego finished off his drink and saddened.
"Sounds like my marriage but with less of the passion."
Marriage is a multiple of two and René realised he was

a remainder. Piece by piece did Diego analyse the slender
        body.
"Do you know what 'synthetic a priori' is?" René shook his
        head.
Diego explained, but his first intuition was to close the
        bedroom door.

## 2. When points belong to something at a fixed time, it is a date.

"Do you always have dinner with your students?"
"The rising stars, yes," said Ruth, confident with no
     wedding ring.
"So, what part of India are you from?"

"I'm a mish-mash: London born, Australia raised. Returned."
"Explains the twang. And the French name? Why Geometry?"
"Parents. Practical romantics. Mathematics. Cold beauty,"
     René said,

hiding truth behind truth.
"Why academia, Ruth?"
"Should I say the joy of knowledge,

I'd be a liar; with all this fucking red tape
I'd have been better off in Westminster –
at least there I could dispense it!"

"Sorry, I've a tutoring session at Clare College now," said
     René. Ruth touched his hand,
"I'm a forward thinker. And forward. We should explore
     discrete mathematics?"
"*Discreet* mathematics."

### 3.   *The marriage bed is a sacred surface.*

"Fancy some hanky-panky?"
"Not now, I have to finish," Ruth said,
combing her way through formulae of space-

time. Minutes passed like an irregular heart-
beat. Tapping a pen, twiddling his thumbs, Diego said,
"Come on. It could be our private *Big Bang*."

"Fine. If it'll make you shut up!"
Ruth threw the marking to the ground.
11.25pm.

11.57pm.
"So, who's Minkowski?" Diego peered at Ruth's papers.
"He developed the space–time continuum."

Ruth looked up. Diego's eyes shone peacock-blue.
"Do you want to hear a story about Time?"
Before Ruth could refuse, Diego began …

## 4.   *Did the imagination conceive Time?*

"What beast is this?!" yelled the villagers.
"Gaze the legendary Phoenix," Orion the hunter said, as
the ensnared bird cried fire.

Orion's desire was an avian exhibit,
bringing joy to the people who lived in
a world still and constant: close to paradise.

But the phoenix grew weak, the crowds grew tired. Frustrated,
Orion wanted worship; God-like status – no! they come
        and go –
A star, heaven set, peach-tinged light burning eternally.

"COME ALL. WITNESS THIS LEGENDARY EVENT.
DEATH OF THE PHOENIX," Orion called.
The people gathered, ravenous for entertainment.

The bird's beak was tarnished copper; feathers of fire were
        weaker than
ash and embers. Her deathbed was a pyre but soon
her body was an arsonist's dream.

People marvelled: from gold bars a new phoenix burst out,
smashing the cage, slices of steel bulleting the crowds.

The phoenix's brilliant plumage blinded Orion instantly.
She circled the world in seconds,
faster than a thought, faster than light, so that when she
        stopped
the world was left spinning:

The seas cried fury in tidal waves; the wind unleashed the
        chaos of weather while
the sun plunged below the horizon, allowing the night's
        bitterness to capture the land-scape: the moon, like an
        invisible pillar supporting the earth, let go and turned
        its back on

us. You. Me, now bound by the perils of age and death. Time
        had begun.

*

"What kind of story was that?" Ruth said, annoyed she hadn't
        finished her marking.
Diego beamed like a wise orator. "I liked it."

"Goodnight." Ruth, eyes closed, a trillion-long to-do list still
        ran through her mind.
And in the blanket of night did Diego whisper,
"Did you come?"

## 5.  "'Bodies in geometric space are subject to linear time.'

Good. Oh, I forgot to ask, how was the conference?" Ruth said,
handing back the first part of René's thesis.

"So, I mistook fourteen thirty for four thirty and ended up in a
    philosophy seminar. I was too embarrassed to leave,"
    said René – omitting Diego, whose beauty made him
    stay.
Hearing this, Ruth broke out into volcanic laughter –

the irony of a PhD student confusing such basic numbers.
"I haven't laughed like that since the nineties," she said.
"What happened in that year?"

"I married." Ruth's face darkened as if she moved from
    sunlight to shade.
René was an interval that linked two wedded people – at least
    Ruth and Diego weren't together. Alone, for certain,
    Ruth locked the door. "Need to be quick – board
    meeting."

She slid out a pin, and her hair, dark as coffee beans, fell to
    her shoulders; a rush,
tangible rapture, as her blouse fell away; they fucked
for exactly 314,159 milliseconds – long enough to feel the
    infinite sense of pleasure.

## 6.   *Memory is a line that repeats upon itself.*

*It's ninety-five, another year gone. I have a part-time boyfriend
        and a failing career;*
*I'm a full-time lecturer going nowhere*, Ruth thought,
        twiddling her azure hoop earring.
"What's on your mind?" Diego said, glancing as the waiter
        bent over.

"Why haven't they given me a professorship yet? Walking on
        the university's grass, for God's sake, is my only
        privilege. I'm a woman; that's why I've been
        overlooked."
"Hang on, Ruth, universities abide by equal opportunities."

"Sure, and the bell curve doesn't exist."
Diego smiled. Never had he met a woman so stunning
        when angry.
"Ready to order?" The waiter scribed their desires.

"Vegetarian."
"Veal."
"Very good."

Both Diego and Ruth watched the waiter's tight arse as he
        walked away.
Ruth thought: *He is …*
*… very tasty*, thought Diego.

In the snap of a poppadum, Ruth realised:
*There's only one way I'll get what I want …*
*He's not that bad. I could do worse.*

'Diego. How long have we dated?"
"About two and a half years. Who's counting?"
"How does Professor Diego Dempewolf sound?"

"Professorships. Tenures. I don't get it." He tried reaching for
        the raita. "Will you—"
"Marry me."
Diego thought *he* should ask that question – because men
        had to, didn't they?

He was as blank as a goldfish. He waited. He watched her
        waiting for his reply.
"What about travel plans? Our trip to India. Buddhist retreats.
        There's still time … Yes."
"Good." Ruth shook his hand, and a complex disaster was
        born.

## 7. *To formulate the proposition.*

"I cut short an important *supervision*." Ruth fanned herself
    with René's folder.
'Direct as always, Doctor Emmy," said Professor Georg,
    chairman. "You look flushed."
"I'm … Just tell me what the hell is going on. There are only
    two reasons you sit

before the board: to be moved,
whether it is promotion or demotion;
either way, you move up or down Cambridge's academic
    ladder."

"Everything is fine. Trust us."
Ruth grimaced; knowing
trust was a precious bird in a lion's jaws.

"Doctor Emmy," said Professor Georg, focusing upon, almost
tasting, the acidity of Ruth's fierce green eyes.
"Hyperbole aside, you're the finest mathematician at this
    university, perhaps the world.

It's time to take your position among Cambridge's academic
    elite. And all
we ask is for you to write another paper this year – a paper to

redefine analytic geometry – and the world will be your
oyster."

"Pearls come at a price."
"Name it."
"Professorship."

## 8.   Theorem: Economic rationalism and philosophy are incongruent.

"What's this all about? There's only one reason you're called before the board: I'm going to be economically mauled!" Diego stood before four suits.

"Doctor Dempewolf, let's not be hasty," said lead-man-in-suit.
One by one, the others nodded as if opinions were a domino
    effect.
"Students want twenty-first century learning: marketing,
    media, social-media."

*Would they be so smug if I mentally undressed them?*
    Diego thought,
analysed: overweight/middle-aged man x 4 = *nasty thought*;
    better left dressed.
"Are we an exam factory? A degree supermarket? When do
    students actually *think*?"

The suits were perturbed. One, duller than wet concrete,
    cleared his throat,
"Very well. Your last article on substance dualism and Theory
    of Mind was fine,
but we wish to make the Philosophy Department more …
    more streamlined."

Diego raised an eyebrow, "How streamlined?"

"The department is to be halved and merged with English and
Media Studies.

Your contract is under review."

## 9.   An acute conversation: speakers are < 90° apart.

"I thought philosophy was an excuse for self-employment,"
    René said,
while Diego traced the endless circumference of his navel.
    René continued,
"What's this about 'are we really here?' I exist. The bed exists.
    End of story."

"But at the sub-atomic level nothing exists." Diego's hand slid
    downwards.
"We're nothing but atoms and starlight. Perception can be as
    abstract as mathematics."
The weight of Diego's concept and hand stunned René and

he tingled with pleasure. "Okay, Doctor Dempewolf, I
    concede. Now I need you to
tell me about love." Diego pondered, adjusted his glasses and
    unbuttoned René's shirt.
"Love is a unique feeling that contours the breadth of life."

"What?"
"Life, René. It's a line with eternal breadth. Relationships
    constantly extend
horizontally – like now." To René's delight, Diego nuzzled
    him with his nose.

On a single bed, single dorm, empty as a cave, they lay.

"Won't you be late for work? Hey, what's wrong?"
Diego pulled René into his arms, this lithe body the most
    concrete thing in his life.

## 10. Memory is a line that intersects with itself.

"And they all lived happily ever after."
"Goodnight, my little Ruthy."
"But look at the clock: two minutes until official bedtime."

"Then you can wake up two minutes early."
"Mummy."
"Yes?"

"I want to be a *math-e-matician*."
"That's a long word for a little girl."
"Numbers are funny fun."

"Then you'll be a telephonist or count
all the babies you'll have. Now go to sleep."
Ruth's mother's kiss was colder than a paperweight.

*

A pencil snapped. Ruth snapped out of her day-
dream. GEOMETRY 112. 3pm.
"Great. Fucking undergraduates."

## 11.  Like formulae, can love be rearranged?

"No. No, Mum, it definitely can't."

"We'll see. So, how was your day, Nay?"

*The joy of small talk,* thought René. "Don't call me that, Mum. It's embarrassing.

Eight hours with a book; bookworm vs. social bug – I know the stronger insect."

"Are you seeing anyone?"

" …

Does it matter?"

"Everything matters. Yasmin waits for you. She moved to Sydney."

"Not that again. How have you been since—"

"I joined a cookery group – there are ladies my age – passes the time."

"Time flies, flees and fights us. See you in a few weeks – conference. Bye."

René sighed, a weary beast on migration. How long could he keep running?

## 12.   "To propose the formula

to give you all the answers. That is why I am here,
        gentlemen."
"We hope so, Dr Dempewolf, the board's time is precious."

"As precious as money. I am here to save philosophy.
I propose a paper to
change our view of Mind–Body dualism.

Trust me, the department will be showered in fame and
        fortune."
"To be blunt, Diego, we don't trust you, so just
deliver, or else …"

## 13.  Indifference: two circles that touch but do not cut one another.

I'm a constant, remaining
unchanged under transformations:
I have married; I have a lover,

yet I am the same as I was
yesterday, two weeks, and twenty years ago –
yes, I am enraged at times, but

deep down, I care little for those
around me. There is a plenitude of concepts, and
theories that need to be tied together – this is all that truly
         matters to me.

My indifference renders me objective;
I am free; I am solid and stable as a tree whose
roots plunge deep into mineral-rich earth.

Ruth pondered as she continued to work on
a theory to shape modern mathematics.

## 14. To go beyond the proposition.

*To be great,*
*to be known, to be*
*the arc in History's path,*

*opening the way for*
*new thought and new ways of being.*
*Impossible*, Diego thought.

*I cannot resolve the duel between mind and body*
*in a month*. A century. A millennia. Time's dream's thief;
how did a promise become a prison?

## 15. Acute memories can permeate 90% of one's life.

René remembered: cramming for exams.
Distant sound: his father grunting, mother weeping.
Tears blur equations.

"Let's go," his father commanded.
"Where?"
"Prayers."

The call to prayer fills the sky like a flock of birds.
The words float into René's ears, but
prayer utters no solace to a heart behind bars.

Moving with the motion of other men,
René has the notion that he must, must, must
flee.

## 16. Definition: Bases are those who support a top.

"And ever since, atheism has been your 'religion'."
"Yes, but there's no breaking cultural shackles – no pork, no
     booze … perhaps a tipple."
"But what stops you if the base of religion is gone?

You don't believe in the fundamentals; why cling to that
     which has no meaning?"
"It's the superficial that holds the most meaning in our lives.
     I'm with you right now –
a meaningless moment," René lied, feeling secure in Diego's
     arms powerful arms,

"and yet we can't live without such simple actions as being
     held or kissed;
I can't rid myself of that which has been ingrained within me.
     Enough philosophy."
"Fair enough … What's inside that diary? You seem to take it
     everywhere with you."

"It's private."
"That's an invitation: others must read it!"
"You'll have to get through me first."

"With pleasure," Diego said,

throwing René down and exploring him like Marlow in the
   Congo.
The diary remained untouched and unseen.

## 17. An idea is that which has depth and a vast length and breadth expandable over the distance of time.

Her office was a universe: bitterly cold; the lamp light was as
    white as onion flesh.
Ruth shivered and rubbed her slender arms. *Algebra is my*
    *needle, language my thread;*
*I shall bind the branches of Mathematics*

*together. Unifying algebra,*
*linear algebra,*
*topology and logic into*

*a body of principles; moreover,*
*I shall reveal the relationship between*
*symmetries in physics and conversation principles,*

*to construct, comparative to human relationships, which,*
*the theory tells us, should be relatively*
*simple.*

## 18.  Let ballet be a mathematical catalyst.


Royal Opera House. From a box, Ruth and René gazed at
her leg forming a triangle in a pirouette, limbs approaching
        infinity;
the ballet even lingered in her fingers: so dexterous and
        determined.


His split leap rested on the edge of perfect precision
and strength to carry dancers and the dance.
His triangular body: a geometric dream.


"The ticket's on me, by the way. Aren't you glad we came?
        Isn't the *prima* gorgeous?
What do you think of her?" Ruth whispered, squeezing
        René's knee.
But René glanced more at the *danseurs* than the dance.


He looked at the two men, the twenty ballerinas blurring into
        pirouettes, and thought:
*One to ten.*
*Desire's ratio.*

### 19. Definition: Body chronology can be unequal to the mind's.

"Your skin is warm, sweeter than molasses," Diego said while
embracing René in front of a full-length mirror,
exploring his body with hands delicate as spiders' feet, but

Diego stopped as he caught a glance at his own reflection.
"What's wrong?"
"René, what am I doing?

I'm old enough to be your father."
"And I'm young enough to be your lover," René said with a sly
     smile.
"So you're older than I am. It only matters if it has any
     meaning, and it doesn't

when the language of love is a language without time;
the generation gap is closed when your lips meet mine."
"You sound like a philosopher. Looks like my work has rubbed
     off on you."

"In the most intimate of places. Come with me.
Love's a verb demanding conjugation." And with that
René led Diego to bed to exercise a different kind of grammar.

## 20. Parallel planes in unparalleled spaces are those which can meet.

"So, you finally decided to call me?"

"You haven't changed a bit, Yasmin."

"Oh yes I have. You swan off to jolly ol' England, no word for

four months, not even a text! Are your thumbs broken or
        something?"

"Exactly. You're always changing, thus you haven't changed."

"So, what have you been up to?"

"Nothing really."

"That's a euphemism for everything. What's going on?"

"You aim the arrow straight for the heart, don't you?"

"Spare me the poetry. Who is she?"

"Um … well, there are two."

"René … twice the lover twice the heartache. You know

your mum keeps on going on about us."

René chuckled, Yasmin did not.

"Strange. You're a continent away, in the middle of nowhere,
        but it feels like

you're right here with me. Well, you know you'll have to let down an unlucky lady."

"Yes. *A lady.*"

## 21. The reconciliation of parallel lines, like opposing concepts, cannot occur.

*Time is water slipping through the fingers of cupped hands:*
       *the bowl of*
*a beggar reaching out for a coin that can buy answers*
*to fix these dilemmas that infest me like maggots chewing the*
       *flesh of fruit.*

*Question: What fuels the mechanisms for reactions in*
       *response to external events?*
*Fuelled by another question: Why do I love men yet need*
       *women?*
*Life is plagued by contraries.* Circles darker than tea beneath
       his eyes, Diego thought:

*if attraction were a type of heat; would it affect the peripheral*
       *ends of our nerve fibrils;*
*would it disturb the space in the pattern of the interfibrillar*
       *space, causing us*
*to react instantly though irrationally as if lust were a reflex*
       *action …?*

Who could ever perceive the end of time?
6.58 am, in a room darker than a starless universe,
Diego's world ended, not with a bang but with a whimper.

## 22. When uneven planes collide, the weaker will no doubt be crushed.

"You haven't delivered, Diego," the head of the board
      snapped.
"You can't rush genius, gentlemen."
"Diego, I've read of monks who have achieved enlightenment
      faster than

you. Produce one paper – how long should it take? Time's
      up."
"What do you mean, *time's up*? This isn't a game show – it's
      my profession."
"We know. You will receive our decision tomorrow." The suits
      left abruptly.

Diego sat, deflated, alone, wanting to punch a wall but
he couldn't. Curse. He couldn't. Cry. He couldn't do
      anything, for
the toxicity of silence hijacked his heart.

## 23. Two points may exist in the same space but not necessarily in the same plane.

"I booked the twelve thirty flight, not the two thirty flight, you
    idiot! Damn airlines."
Ruth slammed the phone down and returned to her research –
    numbers she could control.
She ignored the figure diametrically before her.

At the end of the room Ruth's husband sat, sadder than a cat
    wearing a vet's collar.
"I'm having an affair!" Diego said, to get her attention.
"That's nice, dear," Ruth said, concentrating on equations.

A bee, whose last resort was to sting, Diego shouted:
"I'm about lose my job; I'm having an affair; and that's all you
    can say?!
I could kill myself and you wouldn't care less!"

Ruth's hypnotic green eyes narrowed. "Diego, you knew
this marriage was to help our careers. So, if you'll excuse me,
    I have a plane to catch."
Did Ruth walk violently away, or was it the turbulence in
    Diego's tears?

## 24.  If there is no action a consequence can still occur.

"Any plans, Doctor Dempewolf?" said an administrator, grey
   suit and greyer personality.
"Plans? How can I plan when the department is to be cut in
   half?
Not a few subjects cut savagely in half. Who'll hire me at my
   age?"

"Doctor Dempewolf, a good leader plans in case of disasters."
"Good leaders do not have to slash half their staff. Or worse,
   merge with English!
Where the hell is all the money? Maybe if you took

ten per cent of the Vice-Chancellor's salary the philosophy
   department would survive!"
"Doctor Dempewolf, please settle down. You're being
   irrational."
"I'M NOT BEING IRRATIONAL – MY CAREER IS AT STAKE!"

"In light of recent events …"
"What events?"
"The university suggests you take some time … to rest."

## 25. The line of compassion can filter through a phone call.

"I'm sorry, Diego. What will you do?"
"What can I do?"
"Come away with me.

To Köln – I've a meeting with an architect friend.
He won't admit architecture is mathematics is art.
In his blueprints, my heart hidden in numbers.

"I'm not sure. I need persuading," Diego said in a childish
        voice.
"Then to La Rochelle. You'd wake up to a continental
        breakfast, a continental man."
"Keep talking."

"I'd massage your weary shoulders –
I'd untie your tie, then release your fleshy knots."
"I'm still not sure. René, I need some

time to think. Time to make a few phone calls. I'll call you to
        confirm … perhaps."
Feeling like a chick thrown from the nest, René said, firmly,
        "As a philosopher,
consider: time has no need to eat, breathe and love, but your
        lover does."

## 26. The face of a solid is a surface, but a surface is not necessarily solid.

"Oh, it's you."
"You don't sound too happy to hear me."
"What do you want?"

"Does a mother need an excuse to ring her daughter?"
"No. Sorry. It's been a long day."
"How is Diego?"

"We hardly see each other these days."
"Oh, Ruth, that is a shame. Aren't you tired, dear? Perhaps
    take some time off …
You're twenty in your head but your body won't listen – it'll
    age with or without you."

"Mother, I'm at a crucial stage in my career. Children just
    don't fit into the equation."
"When, then? Children take time, Ruth. It's now or never."
"There is plenty of time."

"Ruth! You can't escape biology, but
biology can escape you. One day you'll wake to find
you won't be able to have children anymore."

Ruth rummaged for a comeback or witticism. She searched
    and searched, only

to find a hollowness beneath her solid exterior;
if her heart were a graph, the truth would begin at zero.

## 27. The line of compassion cannot filter through a phone call.

"No. I'm not leaving Chicago."
"But, Ruth, I need to talk to you. Be with me."
"Why should I?"

"Because I'm going through a rough patch; I need your
      support."
Diego suddenly stopped in thought. "I've always been there
      for you."
"Really? Where were you when I lost—"

"You're never going to let that go."
"No. There are some things you can never forgive,

never forget. I've never let you down,
until now – I have to. It's my career – it comes first."
"It always has," Diego whispered.

"What did you say?"
"Nothing. Enjoy Chicago. I'm sure the cleaner will
find my body if I die."


"For God's sake, guilt won't work. I'll bring you back a
      keepsake."
Diego, although furious, could have sworn

he heard Ruth cry. He had never seen her cry – he never
    would.

*

"Hello, René. Guess who?"
"Deep sexy voice – Diego?"
"Is it too late to come with you?"

## 28.  *Water abstracts the straight line.*

"Isn't La Rochelle beautiful?" René said, gazing out of the
    bathroom window.
"Sure," Diego said, pretending to smile.
"What's wrong, Diego? I thought this trip would cheer you up."

"I had everything ordered. Life, the line that should be
    straight, is now concave."
René moved towards Diego. Kissed him, placed some foam
    on his chin and eyebrows.
"Gold hair and eyes bluer than a blue tang. But a Spanish
    surname?"

"German father; Spanish mother. Let me inside your heart,"
    Diego whispered.
A sigh softer than foam, René said, "I'm not ready …" Then,
    eyes closed, thought,
*Does Love equal penetration? Is touch enough?*

*At times I can feel you pass through the pores of my skin,*
*cut into every layer of skin, muscle, bone and marrow. I*
    *haven't been with many people,*
*but often less is more; the part may sometimes be greater than*
    *the whole.*

Diego's thoughts plunged below his navel.
"How many people have you been with?"
"Just two."

"And who was your first?"
"You."
Silence. Diego kissed René's ear. "Sorry. I don't know what I
    want."

"Then let me be there for you." René squeezed Diego's arm.
A miniature crystal ball fell from Diego's eye, crashing into
    the water – destroying the future: "I think you're in this
    too much."

"What?"
"Nothing."
The water was cooling.

## 29.  *Let Mathematics be the bridge to the Arts.*

René stood before Raphael's *Crucified Christ*,
his face lit with awe, not from painter or paint,
but from the mathematical beauty before him.

Christ's face, angels behind, four people,
who gazed up, knowing he would soon be gone,
construct an invisible decagon.

René saw circles, pentagons and triangles;
these angles and lines formed a tangle of
geometric shapes pleasurable to the mathematical eye.

"Should I tell Diego the truth?" René said out loud,
 following Christ's line of sight, feeling a surge of courage.
*Line and colour persuade me that I too can be heroic*, he
            thought.

Suddenly, René felt two strong hands creep around his waist,
and almost drowned in Diego's deep voice: "What are you
            thinking?"
*I love you*, René thought, but his words were, "Nothing at all."

## 30. *Postulate 1: To calculate lust.*

"How do you want it, baby?"

"Please, spare me the porn talk. Now, I just need to work this
out before we can start.

So, it's two hundred for the hotel room, another forty for the
breakfast bar;

seventy dollars for dinner, twelve dollars for the *necessary items*;
two hundred and fifty for the agency's fee, plus an extra ten per
cent;

plus two hundred to rent your dick. Now, do I need to tip?

How much do you tip in Chicago?"

"Uh …"

"Don't bother, that would mean another five dollars for your
intellect.

So that comes to nine hundred and fifty-seven dollars. Well,
what are you waiting for?"

"You've kind of put me off. I don't think I can … you know."

"Useless. Forget about it. I'll pay the agent's fee."

"Can I still have the breakfast bar?"

Ruth threw a calculator at the escort and
missed by a fraction she dare not calculate.

## 31. Theorem: Love and sex coincide with one another but are not equal.

"René, this is terrible. What's happened to the standard of
    your work?" Ruth said,
glancing over the chapters. René replied, "I'm going through
    a rough patch."
"Still, this is the type of work I'd expect from pathetic
    undergrads. You write about

the postulate of homogeneity without mentioning Delboeuf,
    René.
René! Are you listening to me?!" Ruth yelled.
"What? What did you just say?"

"René, your body is here but you're miles away. Why don't we
    take a rest?"
"How's your husband?"
"Who?"

"Your husband," René asked with a thief's guilt.
"Oh him … alright. Haven't seen him since I returned from
    Chicago."
"Have you told him about us?"

"Oh God no. My hours at work and after work don't concern
    him."
"Do you still sleep together?"

"On and off. Mainly off – the usual state of his libido.
What's this all about, René? Come on. Why don't we go to the
        cinema and
then back to your place? No, let's go straight to your place."
"Not tonight."

"Most men would jump at the chance.
We *could* visit a *seedier* place – see some girls, girls with girls …"
"I'm not most men, and I don't like to watch two girls at it for
        the price of a steak!

Love and sex are indivisible," René said, tenaciously.
"They've got nothing to do with each other."
"You're wrong. Wrong! I'll fix this paper," said René.

Ruth moved towards him, tried to unbutton his shirt, but he
        walked away,
leaving Ruth with one thought:
*Since when did men say no to sex?*

## *32. The past is that which has length and lingers.*

In his office, smaller than a postage stamp, cluttered like a
       flea market,
Diego remembered: a doorbell chime, his father coming
home from work to find the table laid, to be

kissed by his mother, who then served dinner.
His siblings sat with napkins before a meal; saying grace;
hearing the trivialities of a working day; and he pondered:

tragedy is mediocrity.

## 33. Death's axis can be difficult to cross.


Diego had decided.
"It's the best way; a bit too fashionable,
but an easy and feasible task.

Checklist:
Garage door – closed.
Car windows – open."

Diego started the ignition, and waited …
And waited. Struck only by a pounding headache, he
        punched the wheel.
"Fucking unleaded petrol!"

## 34.   Love's only axiom is uncertainty.

Half a year has passed, and I'm halfway through my thesis.
Tomorrow I will visit Ruth.
But tonight I lie here with you,

in my bedroom, filled with the sound of
        Satie's $1^{ére}$ Gymnopédie.
I roll my tongue over you like a ballpoint pen.

I plot kisses down the axis of your spine.
$Y = ax^3 =$ the subtle curve of your hip, held in my hand.

Your body is a solid geometry fundamental in my world.
Diego suddenly awoke like a scared child and said to René,
"I wanted to … to let go of life last night."

## 35. $L (\in) = K \in {}^{1\text{-}D^*}$

René just stared at the formula.

*Bend towards me.*
*I am a body geometrist*
*analysing the lines of your lips.*
*Kiss me. Our tongues move in synchrony,*
*in ephemeral ∈ternity.*
*But minus me from you is to Destroy us.*
*How are reciprocal bonds held*
*together? This vigour for each other*
*creates ∈ternal fuel, carrying us*
*beyond lust, past beauty's boundaries; Thus,*
*L = Love.*

## 36.   *For every triangle there is a sin.*

"The doctor said to stop moping, Diego! Please, I'm expecting
a visitor."
Moments later came a knock at the door. Ruth answered and
led René
into the living room. Diego jumped to his feet. "René!" he said
with alarm.

"How do you know René?" Ruth asked Diego.
"He's my lover," Diego blurted out.
"Diego! What are you doing here?" René asked.

"He's my husband," said Ruth, ruthlessly.
"A word, Diego. Now!"
Inside the kitchen, spotless and unused, Ruth yelled, "What the
fuck are you playing at?!"

"You answered your own question. Don't give me that look of
ultimatum," said Diego.
"I'd be happier if you were sleeping with a woman. Are you …?"
"Does it matter? I'd be happy with a bloody dog but you've said
no to pets. We're

together alone in this jail of a marriage." Diego left the house.
René couldn't stop him.

Ruth, viciously vexed, came out and said, "Philosophers blow
things out of proportion."
René knew this: Love's hyperbole, but he daren't say it aloud.

## 37. The axiom of decision can only be made in fixed space and time.

"How can I help you?" Professor Georg led René into an office,
every square inch of wall space crammed with books, piles of
       text-
books, that became a maze René wove through, careful not to
       topple any.

"I'm not sure this is for me," said René, noting a moth hole in
       Georg's polo shirt.
"Whatever for? You're doing so well. Ruth tells me you're a
       rising star – few have
a full scholarship at Cambridge. The name alone will open
       doors. Aren't you settled yet?"

"I'm more the rogue planet. *Planetos* in the true sense:
       wandering the sky."
"Tell me, why are undertaking a massive task like a PhD, then?"
René remembered an exact moment

in his bedroom, trying to block out the sound of his mother
       yelling on the phone.
Staring at the computer – a myriad of university websites –
avoiding the medical pages due to family pressure. Clicked a
       hyper-
link to another page. Philosophy Department. A photo
       stopped René from blinking.

'The Mind and Embers: A Conference', René read, then gazed
　　　　at the image of a man:
a jaw borrowed from a dragon, eyes set like lapis lazuli gems.
　　　　Hard, fast, he fell …


　　　　　　　　　　　*


"… In love with mathematics, I guess." René couldn't look
　　　　Georg in the eye.
"Well, why quit when you're nearly at the finish line?
　　　　Stressed. Take a few days to
clear your head, and give my *regards* to Ruth," said Professor
　　　　Georg.

## 38.  *New angles change perspective.*

"So, what's he like in bed?" said Diego, stepping out of the
     shower and into the bedroom.
"You tell me." Ruth glared at Diego from her vanity mirror.
"*Touché*. So now there is privacy within our private life,"
     Diego said, vindictively.

"Will you continue to see him?" Diego towelled his hair.
"Will you?" Ruth gazed at her naked husband, the solidity of
     his body alien to her.
"Look, we're running around in circles here."

"Now you know how I've felt since I married you." Ruth
     snapped her compact shut.
"You really don't care about me, do you?"
"Grow up, Diego. I care, I guess, but not for every
     microsecond of the day!

Anyway, straight – you're obviously not – when did you meet
     him?"
"Does it matter? Can't I be curious? You know nothing in
     nature is ever 'straight'."
"You were always good at hiding behind philosophy."
     Nostalgia offered Ruth a grin.

"We met in July when he missed the Dimensions of
     Pythagoras conference."

"You're wrong; that conference was in November, Diego. I
put it my own diary."
"What? Something doesn't add up." An imbalanced equation
left Diego with

a negative feeling.

## 39. And deception is the centre of silence.

"The facts, René! How could you end up at the wrong
        conference, when
your conference was four months away? Now, I'm no
        Einstein, no Benoit Mandelbrot,
no Euclidean genius, but it doesn't take a genius to work out
        that

you didn't arrive by accident. Did you? How the hell did you
        even find out
I would be there, the room number? … I guess you even
        knew my hotel suite.
Have you been stalking me? How many more lies are there?

Say something! Hang on. Perhaps I'm blowing things out of
        proportion.
Perhaps you were there by chance, and took the caution of
        not telling me the truth
to save face. After all, a mathematician who forgets dates –
        funny. It worked on me.

It worked well in my bed too! Or were you after sex? I don't
        blame you for that;
what woman or man could resist me? But no, you said you'd
        take care of me.

Is this care, then? Deceit. Don't look at me like that! Say
    something, René!

Are you just going to stand there? Statue silent. Are you too
    guilty to speak? Why?
Why? Oh, I see, you probably had a good laugh with Ruth.
    Damnit! Say something."
Before leaving, René placed a diary between Diego's legs:

his place of thought.

# Poetics of a Mathematician

By René Ali

## *I.*

*Mathematical certainty let it be,*
*but when love and math collide*
*one plus one can equal three.*
*And so if one is to decide*
*between a woman or a man,*
*there is no procedure, technique,*
*equation, method, or grand plan*
*to avoid a predicament that is not bleak.*
*Thus, I am to reveal my disastrous life*
*now bound to a bittersweet triangle*
*(the reason I've neither husband nor wife).*
*Perhaps these pages will disentangle*
*doubt, as I expand, subtract, use addition*
*to expose the thoughts of a mathematician.*

## II.

During my undergraduate days,
I studied calculus – a minor – now used
to calculate my erroneous ways.
My fellow peers all oozed
into a world of casual sex,
predicting if I'd sway their way,
like the regression of Y on X.
But my heart had the final say,
with no warning my body did fall
into the call of Romantic love,
spinning like a roulette ball,
I was confused and innocent of
Love's pitfalls and indeed the worst,
but let me tell you about my first.

## III.


*Crush. While in a ninth-grade English class,*
*reading* The Passionate Pilgrim, *I saw a girl*
*whose hands were like delicate Venetian glass,*
*and skin that glowed like mother-of-pearl.*
*I longed to hold her slender hips, and glide*
*my tongue across her lips, so I sat beside her*
*to ask if she would tutor me (of course I lied).*
*(Sorry, her name was Angela Esquer).*
*At her house, she told me stories to delight my ear,*
*but when her six-foot-four brother said hello on the occasion,*
*I felt a rush and trill like the eve of the New Year,*
*realising men would be a part of my sexual equation.*
*So reading this, you now understand and see*
*that triangles are not entirely new to me.*

*IV.*


*I didn't date Angela, despite my crush,*
*"The territory of love is so immense;*
*plenty of time for love – no need to rush,"*
*my father said, sounding like he made sense.*
*Marriage? Love? It's a simple crush, I thought.*
*My father: mean and religiously devout,*
*selfish and stubborn – qualities all self-taught.*
*But he was never abusive, nor did he scream or shout.*
*(Why do we hate those who do no wrong?)*
*I believe I hated him for loving me*
*to the point of controlling me all day long.*
*I wanted to flee: Michigan, Montreal or Maebashi.*
*However, I defied my father by not becoming a surgeon,*
*though I obeyed one law: I remained a virgin.*

## V.

*For so long I abstained from intercourse.*
*The order: marriage, children, then perhaps sex,*
*laid down before me. My dad would, of course, enforce*
*the rule. But I broke it, for life has a googolplex*
*of trapdoors and backdoors to escape. For on my*
*graduation night I hatched a plan to help me flee.*
*(I would not study medicine, but instead apply*
*for post-graduate studies in the US or the UK possibly.)*
*As I received my degree, Dad's heart decided to stop –*
*died of a stroke as soon as the paper touched my hand.*
*There was mass panic, my mother hysterical non-stop.*
*But I was stone still and felt somewhat like Macbeth,*
*for what monster could take such pleasure from death?*

## VI.

An opportunist. That is what I am,
as tragedy bore opportunity;
my mindset like a cartogram:
the UK was the place to be!
Although my mother pleaded,
"Study but at least stay in Adelaide,
this is your home and where you're needed."
But it was too late – the decision made.
(I'd also applied for a scholarship –
a safety net for five whole years.)
It was hard leaving Mum, but I bit my lip,
held back my tears and faced my fears,
for a kingdom awaited me
with a lone person I longed to see ...

## VII.

Fitting it should rain when
I landed in this grey landscape.
The drizzle did not dampen my acumen
into these plans which were shipshape,
and ready to be put into action.
I bathed in limitless pleasure,
a perfect plan like a balanced fraction –
precise, concise and suffice so that leisure
time could be mine. However, my room:
emptier than a monastery.
But I relaxed, lay down, listened to Strauss
and enjoyed this domestic effrontery.
I was a little worried, to tell the truth,
for tomorrow I'd be meeting Ruth.

## VIII.


*"I hope you've settled in alright;*
*a few months and you'll be acclimatised."*
*"I'm fine, though the traffic keeps me up at night."*
*"Yes, it looks like you've been anaesthetised.*
*Take this – it might help your thesis."*
*"Conferences: 'Dimensions of Pythagoras',*
*'Descartes: Mind and Body in Pieces'.*
*How intriguing and adventurous!*
*What's this?" "'The Mind and Embers'.*
*That's Philosophy – you needn't go.*
*Descartes is this week; Dimensions in November;*
*Here's some references you'll need to know."*
*I couldn't care, for in my hands I had the key*
*for you to take and unlock me …*

*IX.*


*You led me through a swarming crowd*
*which, like clouds, had descended, to rain*
*questions upon you. But they were becloud*
*as you said aloud, "Must dash. Here, have some champagne!"*
*You took me through a maze*
*of endless corridors that coiled like a*
*spring. Seasons of longing left me ablaze*
*with anticipation.* So here is the moment, René,
*I said to myself as you turned the lock,*
*and I stepped into the den of desire*
*and into a new world and epoch*
*that is passion charged like a live wire.*
*For this was no one-night stand you could ignore*
*as you closed the bedroom door.*

**X.**

Unclothed and beneath the covers
we conversed about the concepts of beauty:
two men together: symmetrical lovers;
touch: beauty's language, and our duty
in order to communicate. These notions
blew me away as you say you'd love
to climb a live volcano – a characteristic of
stupidity, though a spectacle – flaming oceans!
You are a volcano – dormant but now awake;
you glazed my body with your saliva-like lava,
massaged me with the strength to make a continent ache.
The pounding blood of your veins, vessels and vena cava
urges me to abseil down your abdomen, heading south
to feel Vesuvius explode in my mouth.

## XI.

*Evening. And all I saw was your silhouette*
*pressed upon me. You said, "You cannot subtract*
*mind from body – they're locked in eternal duet."*
*"But how is one to unlock them?" I react.*
*Your hands circled and slid down*
*my body like an ice-dancer's blade:*
*erogenous silence. There is no noun*
*to describe this pleasure that doesn't fade.*
*It is the reflection that is the key,*
*man to man unlocks desire – I agree!*
*For the body is familiar; touch: genuine and true,*
*our minds free to wonder. Thus, I thank you,*
*for you let me into the secret, my lover,*
*of what men can do to each other.*

*XII.*

*In low registers, your voice lurks,*
*warming me in your embrace.*
*"We are all bound to frameworks."*
*You said, "The cycle of seasons; space–*
*time traps us into the struggle of life and death;*
*and memory is tied to chronology."*
*I feel light-headed and out of breath,*
*for I could only use seismology*
*to measure the impact of your words upon*
*my mind. Though filled with awe and packed*
*with pleasure, a thought makes me react,*
*how would I cope if you were to subtract*
*me for another. And I was suddenly aware:*
*relationships are indivisible by three. I must prepare.*

## XIII.

*"Because my heart is weak and cannot withstand*
*the thought of you leaving me," I said to myself*
*while in the bath, while hearing you hum – Streisand? –*
*as you shave. I peer over to see an abundant wealth*
*of muscles and angles – geometric bliss. (You turn and I'd love*
*to measure the circumference of your crown, my king!)*
*Beneath the water, I wonder if we are like a hand to a glove?*
*Perfect and prepared for what the future may bring.*
*No. Because you are like analytic geometry:*
*numbers can show your position in space,*
*thus you're with Ruth when not with me – which I cannot face.*
*My heart's not strong enough to share you. Tacheometry:*
*I contemplate the measurement of distance: every minute, hour,*
*I will watch you like sentinels from a watchtower.*

## XIV.

With all that has happened, please realise this,
I meant to hurt and cause you grief
for life cannot be lived in eternal bliss
as such a life is a life of false belief.
My desire is to only be with you – a cliché,
I know. I have slept with your wife
to cause your marriage to decay,
in order for you and I to share a life.
You show me concepts to fill me with awe;
a constant force to fuel my mind
with motion, you're my Newton's first law.
How can I untangle that which is intertwined?
How could I leave when you have shown me
a love to break all form and structure?

## 40.  *The action cannot be undone.*


"My name is drunk, and my Diego's left his wallet at home."
"Sir, I think you've had—"
"Enough of work, love and life. Let me give you, yes you, some

advice: two relationships can't be balanced at once."
"Perhaps you need another drink."
"No. Got to stop spinning," Diego said, clutching René's diary
        that touched his heart,

yet couldn't stop him from thinking of Ruth.
Solidity: marriage vows. "She's my only certainty in life." And
        Diego walked away from the the diary with all its

passion left behind.

## 41. The diameter of decision can encompass a whole life.

Eleven pm. Ruth sat in Georg's office. Conversations and
laughter. Empty glasses.
Merlot. Malbec. Shiraz. Sangiovese. Cabernet Sauvignon.
Rioja. Zinfandel. Pinot Noir. Pinot Grigio. Never mix
wines – they didn't care!

Ruth tilted her head back, her hair falling like a spill of coffee,
groaning. "When?!"
"The board needs to approve promotions. Time, give it time,
Ruth."
In the awkward silence, Ruth gazed at Georg and compared
him to Diego.

Georg: Broad-shouldered. He was not. Tall.
He was not. Well dressed. His gangly frame looked allergic to
gyms.
Yet the inexplicable laws of attraction, uninvited, strayed into
Ruth's head.

Georg caressed Ruth's freckled cheek and leaned in.
Ruth felt Georg's breath on her neck, and when he said, "Are
you sure?"
Her common sense screamed *NO* yet the smallest filament of
desire said …

"YES."

## 42. Once bisected a life cannot be reconnected.

*The rain is sharp. Water-*
*drops lacerate my skin. Rain bullets the River Cam. Do rivers*
     *feel pain?*
*What if I were to …*

*Oh, look! Is that Ruth in her car?*
*That seems like René popping into Fitzbillies café, perhaps to*
     *try a Chelsea bun.*
*I will. No, I won't say hello. I need to think. Nothing makes*
     *sense …*

*Does Ruth love me? Does René? Am I capable of loving?*
*Why is Love an irrational number? It can never be divided*
     *easily;*
*there is always a remainder; a messy quotient refusing to be*
     *silent.*

*I must be rational. I must think objectively. What use am I?*
*A soon-to-be-out-of-work philosopher. Even unemployment*
     *laughs at me.*
*Ruth won't stay with me. Will Rene? Do I really want him? But*
     *what if I were to …*

"Diego, how are you?"
"Oh, Georg. Yes. Yes, been never better."

"You mean *never been better*. No punting today, hey. Isn't it a
        beautiful river?


There've been a few accidents; deep or shallow, the water's
        dangerous."
Georg tapped Diego on the shoulder. "Diego. Diego,
        everything all right?"
"Height. Concrete water could smash me to pieces.


What? Oh, sorry, Georg. I'm fine."
"Very well. Must dash. Say *hello* to Ruth."
"If I see her," Diego said, quietly.


As Georg jogged away, Diego spotted the emerald cross of a
        pharmacy –
not the red crosses that plagued his marking, his life –
to care, comfort and cure without a single side effect.

## 43. Proposition: Ratios of difference may sometimes be equal.

"I need to speak to Diego."
"Careful, René, people may start calling you blunt. Come in, and close the door behind you."

"Well, where is he?"
"I don't know. He said he needed time to think. Meet some
contacts for potential jobs.
I haven't seen him in days. And to be honest, I'm exhausted
by it all."

"Why aren't you worried? Why haven't you called the
police?!"
"He needs time to cool off. And why are you in such a hurry
to hunt him down?"
"Because … Why does he need cooling off?"

"We had a little skirmish. Jealously got the better of him, and
rage the best of me;
he was fine after the stitches came out. Then he took off
without a word."
"What?! What the hell did you do to him?"

"Everything he possibly deserved … You look handsome
when angry."
"We *should* be looking Diego."

85

"For God's sake. The man's a homing pigeon. Am I supposed
        to put my life on hold?"

"I can't believe this. I'm going to look for him," René said, but
before he could run out, Ruth intercepted,
"You make a fine mistress, René."

## 44. If the interval is prolonged indefinitely, the given points may never meet.

"... Thank you, Georg, I can't wait to become a professor. Hold on, there's another call.

Hello, Doctor Emmy speaking."

"I knew you wouldn't use your married name. Dempewolf not good enough?

I'm in a miserable hotel. My head and heart are blank. There's no reason to go on."

"Don't be stupid. Give me the address and I'll come pick you up."

(Silence) "Ruth, I don't care about René, I just need ..." Diego wept.

"You're being melodramatic, Diego. Come home and we'll talk about it."

"I need to know. Do love me? Do you?"

"Diego, hold on a minute. I've got to check the other line."

"DON'T PUT ME ON HOLD!"

Ruth ended her call with Professor Georg, then went back to Diego.

"Diego, pick up the phone, this isn't funny ... Diego!"

She heard a painful sigh; a ceased breath.

## 45.   Postulate: Death is disclosed.

"Is it true? What I've read in the *Cambridge News*? Is it true?"
"Yes. It's all true."
"When's the funeral?"

"Two weeks from today."
"You will attend."
"No."

René gripped the phone tight; forearm veins almost bursting
    with rage.
"He was your husband. You have to go!" Ruth stopped him
    like a red traffic light.
"I don't have to do anything. If you think I'm playing the
    grieving widow then forget it!

He was an asswipe. I married him to further my career, that's
    all. And now he's gone, I'm going to move on with my
    life. I suggest you do the same."
"What about us?"

*"What about us?"*
"I see, being cold and callous is your coping mechanism. If
    we're to play that game then I was only with you
    because you're the easiest screw on campus.

Not that the sex was any good. I've slipped into pyjamas
        tighter than you!"
"You always did like tight things, like my husband's ass! You
        fucking fag."
"Oh, so I fuck therefore I am. Well, whatever I do behind the
        bedroom door

at least I loved. Yes, that's right, I loved him!"
"You now know what women go through! And I *won't* be
        dragged into it."
"Don't you dare make this about gender. Love doesn't give a
        fuck about

what's between your legs. It's trivial. It's the connection.
        Closing distance.
Take care of yourself, Ruth – no one else will," René said, and
        hung up.
Ruth wept until her body ached; René halted in revelation.

In his bedroom, narrow as an artery, surrounded by the quiet
        comfort of books,
René let the phone fall on his bed, where it lay, warm like
a heart but without a beat.

## 46. Equal circles are those whose interests are parallel and unconflicting.

"I've just heard some wonderful news! The board is dazzled
      by your work."
"So, will they give me professorship, Georg?"
"Probably an honorary chair at this rate.

Welcome to an elite circle, Ruth," Professor Georg said with a
      little too much excitement.
"Will you stop by the golf club next week? All of management
      will be there, and
they're eager to meet you but … did you need time off?"

"Don't worry, I'll be there," Ruth said, knowing she had to
      take the opportunity.
"Well, I must dash, but stop by my office, and we'll … *talk
      more in depth*."
The time would soon be at hand. Ruth felt a rush knowing only

time was a barrier to her dreams.

### 47. A plane angle is the inclination of two lines in a plane which meet one another, do not lie in a straight line, but lie in sympathy.

"And I've been voted treasurer of the Ladies' Cookery Society; I've never been so busy."

"Sounds ... sounds great."

"You sound lost. Is something wrong? Can I help?"

"Can you bring back the dead?"

"Oh dear, who was it?"

"A friend. A *special* friend. Mum, it's made me think about death. Tell me,

how did you feel when Dad died? Be honest." A silence of six seconds.

"... Your father was a strict man, standing solid in his way, and of course I was upset."

"BE HONEST."

"René, it was the happiest day of my life. Gosh, that sounded terrible."

"I see."

"You don't understand. God lets women live longer than men for a reason.

I dedicated my life to your father and to raising you, and I wouldn't give that up,

but now it's my time to live. My little Nay, I hear you crying."
"Sorry. I'm a mess, numb. My life feels disconnected. Did you
    love Dad?"

"I understood him. It's the same, but it takes longer.
Let's speak of something brighter. How is your doctorate?"
"It's being reviewed. That's why I rang – I'm sending you a
    ticket."

"Oh René, you shouldn't have. Perhaps I'll stop in with family
    in London too."
René's mother could roll out opportunity like roti and feed
    masses.
"Are you seeing anyone?"

René did not respond. His mother spoke as soft as dew on
    grass blades,
"You don't have to say it. I *know*."

## 48. The discourse of mathematics and medicine may conflict.

Ruth sat before her GP, incredulous. "What?! You're joking!"
"This isn't a joking matter."
"But it can't be possible."

"Mrs Dempewolf—"
"Ms Emmy. Doctor Emmy."
"Sorry, Doctor Emmy, the results are positive."

"I had my last test twenty-one days ago, and nothing came
          up. There could be
a three per cent margin of error, perhaps."
"We don't make errors," the doctor said, certain yet snide.

"Listen, medicine like maths is plagued with errors. Human,
          numerical, data;
it all starts from a hypothesis – a stab in the dark." The doctor
          rolled his eyes at Ruth.
"Oh, I see, you think this problem has made me irrational;
          well, I'll show you rational."

"Doctor Emmy, where are you going?"
"A second opinion," Ruth said, and was then stopped dead by
the weight of the situation: "Pregnant."

## 49.   *The final postulate cannot be proven.*

Ruth placed a purple orchid by Diego's headstone.
"I wasn't sure what to bring. I'm terrible with flowers.
Since when did plants have to match our personalities?

Things have changed. And everything I've ever wanted
      changed in the blink of an eye.
They say we shouldn't speak ill of the dead but I fucking hate
      you right now.
I hate you so much.

Yet somewhere in that hate there's a grain of love, and
a grain is all it takes to keep loving you. And I do, I do …
love you …

Love is an equation we can never solve. So why do we keep
      trying?
Does the answer contain the formula for the perfect life?
      Perfect wife, husband, children: what happens after the
      happily ever after?

I quit my job today."

At a crowded airport gate, René sat people-watching. A ticket
        to Australia in hand.

He opened a notebook and wrote: 'Professor Ruth Emmy
        moved to another university.

I completed my PhD, and it is dedicated to you, Diego.

On the first page there is a quote.

Something you once said; something I will always remember:

## 50.    *A life is a line with eternal breadth.'*

Talim Arab was born in London and grew up in Queensland, Australia. His poetry was Highly Commended by the *Arts Queensland Thomas Shapcott Poetry Prize* for an Unpublished Manuscript and received third place in the *Arts Queensland Val Vallis Award* for an Unpublished Poem; he won the *State Library of Queensland's Young Writers Award* (2006). He was also shortlisted for *The Guardian/4th Estate BAME Short Story Prize*. Talim Arab is a Fellow of the Royal Academy of Arts.

Also by Talim Arab:
*The Square-Shaped Tear*